The Tiny Home Guy:

The Life Behind Him

The Tiny Home Guy: The Life Behind Him

Copyright ©2022 by Ron Blair

All rights reserved, which includes the right to reproduce this book or portions thereof in any form whatsoever except as provided by the U.S. Copyright Law.

Published by Petra Publishing House

www.petrapublishinghouse.com

Dedications

Most importantly, my mother, the originator, Vicki Blair

Mike Blair, my brother

My children, Demi Blair, DeAunna Blair, Blake Austin Blair and Dustin Dietzman

Special dedication to Colleen Sandberg, special friend and colleague. Couldn't have done it without you. I miss you and I will never forget you!

Special thanks to HGTV Pie Town Productions for airing the Christina and Hannah episode program before Colleen's return to God.

Christina Latson and daughter Hannah Sebby, my life's better with you in it.

Lou Malang, friend and mentor

Blair's I-5 RVs at Exit 88 in Rochester, WA, 100% sponsors for the tiny home movement (i5rvs.com)

Travis Higgins, top-level authority land development compliance for all levels concerning ADU community developments and tiny homes

Bret and Fysah Sands, "besties." Thanks for the tiny home theme songs and jingles. (FYSAH.com)

Pavel Zagorodnyy, tiny home master craftsman builder

Alexandra Streminski, personal executive administrative assistant

The flock of "Blair's Angels"

Jerry Reeves, friend, world-famous structural engineer, timeless home builder and developer

And of course, the best for last—my publisher Petra Nicoll, author of *Petra's Ashes* and *The Billionaire* series

Table of Contents

Chapter 1: The Fur Coat	1
Chapter 2: Little Blair	7
Chapter 3: Money Mindset	13
Chapter 4: The Wild West	24
Chapter 5: Losing Religion	34
Chapter 6: The Fixer	40
Chapter 7: Mid-Century Milestones	47
Chapter 8: Becoming the Tiny Home Guy	56
Chapter 9: Colleen	63
Chapter 10: Ken Con	71
Chapter 11: Envisioning the Future	76
Chapter 12: What the Family Thinks	81

Chapter 1:
The Fur Coat

Las Vegas is full of all kinds of freaks. Sometimes, I'm one of them. I was in the City of Sin on business. My company was exhibiting a tiny home for Cowboy Christmas at the Convention Center. Ours was the only tiny home on display at what is known as the Super Bowl of rodeos. I was surrounded by thousands of cowboys, cowgirls and chaos.

I assume that the Las Vegas show ended early so exhibitors and visitors alike had more time to gamble. Well, I'm not a gambler so I packed up my belongings to head back to my hotel room on the other side of the strip. I reached for my trademark accessory: my full-length fur coat, which I bought from one of my girlfriend's friends, a hunter/survivalist who needed money. I paid $400 for it but it has given me millions of dollars' worth of opportunity and priceless memories—especially in Vegas, where I could wear it along the strip and be mistaken for a Rod Stewart impersonator and get the girls to pay me for a kiss. Anyway, it kept me warm as I walked from hotel to hotel.

I'm a people watcher and of course, in my fur coat, people were watching me as well. While passing through the

Cosmopolitan Hotel's lobby, I tried not to make eye contact with a guy who had started walking in my direction. It was no use. He approached me and said, "Hey dude, how you doing?" I took two steps back, thinking, *weirdo alert.*

I replied, "I'm doing fine, how are you?" He said, "You don't remember me, former manager of Guns N' Roses"? I said, "Oh, how are you?"- while thinking, *I wonder who I'm supposed to be?* I don't know any former manager of Guns N' Roses. But we got to talking and he asked, "What are you up to?" I said, "Oh, I'm doing a show here for tiny homes." "Tiny homes?" he said. "I got property in Hawaii and I would love to put a tiny home in Hawaii." I replied, "Well, we can do that, I've got a dealer in Hawaii."

We talked a bit more before he said, "You know what? I haven't seen you for so long. Let's go upstairs. I'm buying." And I'm thinking, *Upstairs? What's upstairs?* Always game for adventure, I went with him over to the glass elevator and we rode up to the top floor, not knowing what I was getting myself into.

The elevator opened up right into a high-style bar. This was where the elite meet to eat. About five bartenders, a couple of waitresses, and maybe thirty other people were in the room. They all turned toward the elevator at the same time. You could have heard a pin drop when I walked into the bar. I could feel everyone's stares and hear their thoughts, *Oh my God, who's that guy?* Not too many guys are sporting fur coats, even in Las Vegas. I figured they were thinking I was either a pimp or a rock star!

Finally, someone said, "I thought you left." And he replied, "Nope, I'm buying drinks for everyone." I don't know if the people there were friends of his, but they were for now. Now, I don't normally drink, but I certainly know how. That day, I drank. Everyone there drank because he was buying. We were taking tequila shots and my body temperature started to rise and the fur coat came off. That's when he started having some fun with me. He told everyone that I was a nine-degree black belt, like he is, in four different martial arts. I thought, *Oh dam, this is going to get ugly because I ain't none of that.*

Once I get to drinking, I'm invincible. When I'm in that frame of mind, it doesn't matter how big I am or anyone else is, I can throw stuff around. I was sitting next to my new friend at the bar, and we were wrestling around. Next thing I knew, he grabbed me by the arm, my heart started racing and I thought, *Oh god, here we go.* But he said, "Hey buddy, let's take some selfies." *I thought - this is getting really awkward.* The night went on and on. We drank until we just couldn't drink anymore. The bartenders were drinking, the waitresses were drinking, everyone was drinking as much as they could, because hey, he was buying. I don't know how many people it would have taken to throw me out of that bar but I know how many they intended to use. It was time to go!

Finally, I left and it was the next day, I was told. I thought, *wow, that was weird.* I went back to my room and Googled him to find out he really was a former manager of Guns N' Roses. I still wasn't sure who the hell I was, however. A couple of days went by and I called him back, he had given me his number. We stayed in touch over the next month or so, working on getting him a tiny home in Hawaii. And then finally, I said, "Come on now, you know I'm not whoever it was you thought I was when we met in Las Vegas. Who did you think I was?" He admitted, "Hell, I didn't know you from Adam, but if some guy is wearing a fur coat in Vegas, I want to know who he is."

We became friends after that; we were like brothers from other mothers for a while. I welcomed him into my life. He called me once to tell me he was coming to Washington on his way up to Canada, doing a talent recruitment tour. I gave him an idea of how to market the tour. Aside from my fur coat, another way I attract a lot of attention is by driving around my tiny home. I figured he could benefit from doing the same.

I met up with him at my RV dealership in Rochester, Washington (now called Tiny Homes of the World). We hooked up one of my tiny homes to his BMW SUV with a laminated sign on the back that said, "Talent Search, call this number if you want to be a Rockstar." The tiny home also had my business information, which I thought could help me out, too. Well, it did end up attracting attention—sometimes of the unwanted variety.

This gentleman was a little bit kinky. I decided to drive him to Seattle, where he was going to pick up his girlfriend at the airport, but he wanted to stop at Love's Pantry to get a couple of items first. He assured me it would just be a few minutes, so we triple-parked the Tiny Home Tour Bus that was pulling my tiny home in front of Love's. With my company name plastered on the tiny home and the tour bus, everyone knew it belonged to me—and I was the one waiting, triple parked, while he did his shopping - for two hours. People started showing up, curious about the tiny home. I started giving tours, right there in front of the sex shop.

Finally, I went inside the store and said, "Hey, come on man, doesn't your girlfriend's flight arrive soon?" He appeared distant as he was reading the fine print on a package, then muttered, "Oh, we're just about ready." It took three female staff members to carry his purchases outside. He spent around $4,000 on things I didn't even know existed. They began stuffing everything inside the tiny home; his multitude of porn purchases made it, as they say in Las Vegas, a full house.

We drove to the airport and met up with his girlfriend. Back in the car, we got to talking about the little pit stop at the Love Shop we'd made along the way. His girlfriend said, "Who in the hell do you think you're going to try that shit on?" "It ain't me," she added. I thought to myself, *this is awkward.*

We had made arrangements to stay in a hotel near the airport. We navigated our way through the narrow driveway, not built to accommodate a vehicle of this size

- let alone a tiny home. I then parked the tiny home in the lot. It wasn't until the next morning that I found out he had opened about $1,000 worth of product and strewn everything throughout the tiny home (looking for a few specific gadgets to bring in and no doubt try to persuade his partner to become friends with). Those boxes were pretty graphic. They showed all of it, whatever "it" was. And, he'd left the windows open. Now, as I mentioned—tiny homes attract attention. Everyone that passes has to look inside; it has some sort of magnetic force. Whoever peeked inside sure got a show.

They didn't make it past Bellingham, Washington with his tour. He and his girlfriend got in a fight—but that's a whole other story. I eventually got my tiny home back, but it needed quite a bit of tidying up!

Just another day in the life of "The Tiny Home Guy." A little bit quirky, a little bit kinky and a little bit..... Rock n' Roll.

Chapter 2:
Little Blair

Some of my earliest memories are from living in a tiny home. Not the mobile tiny homes of today—this one was a literal tiny home, located at RAF Mildenhall Air Force base, about eight miles north of London, England. I was around seven years old and my parents were both in the Air Force. I had one older brother and one younger brother; each of us was five years apart.

We lived in a one-bedroom unit on-base, with an open kitchen and area room. My mother remembers those years vividly. I just remember it being a tight space for three kids and two adults, even though it often felt like only one adult lived there since our father was never home. He was a sergeant, working directly under the general and an alcoholic. When he was home, he'd be fighting with my mom. As a child, I got used to a constant roar in the background.

After England, we moved to Wiesbaden, Germany, and my memories there are more vivid. It was 1963, the year the Rhine River froze over. My dad drove a Mini Minor at the time (back before there were Mini Coopers) and I remember him driving it across the river—the ice was that thick. Barges and small ships became stranded in the middle of the river. That was the same year President Kennedy was assassinated. I heard his assassination announced over the loudspeakers while I was at a movie theater.

Back then, kids could navigate throughout the base without parental supervision. I used to entertain myself by taking tours of different castles. As a boy who liked adventure and revenge, the story that stands out the most in my memory was about Mouse Tower, a stone tower on a small island in the Rhine. The legend goes that Hatto II, a cruel ruler who oppressed and exploited the peasants in his domain, was besieged by an army of mice while at his castle. The mice swarmed him as he tried to get to the tower by boat, assuming that the mice couldn't swim. But the mice followed him, swimming into the river by the thousands. When he reached the tower and tried to seek refuge inside, the mice ate through the doors and proceeded to eat Hatto II alive.

I was always very mischievous; that was a blessing for me and a curse for others. I would have loved to have stirred up trouble among the ancient towers and castles in the area, but I was mostly content to find trouble in my own backyard—like that one time when I tried to ignite the nursery on fire. The building was conveniently located next door to our base housing. My older brother, Michael, was always the good guy. He wanted nothing to do with the shenanigans I got into with other base kids. I remember him casually playing on the swings when he said, "You guys shouldn't do that, and you're going to get in trouble. The military police are going to come." Sure enough, the military police came. The rest of us all ran away, but my brother was still there, swinging on the swings, because he hadn't done anything wrong. Well, they arrested him, because he was the only one there, and they took him to the children's jail. He was released, of course, but he wasn't too happy about being wrongly arrested.

In 1965, we moved back to the U.S, first to Auburn, Washington, and then to Tacoma, where we planted roots. We moved into the house that my mother still lives in today. My dad had his Mini Minor shipped over, and he started selling new Ford cars like 1965 Mustangs.

I had calmed down a little by then but was still a little bit mischievous. I think I got that side from my dad; or at least, he contributed to it by never being around. I think I tried to fill the void his absence caused in my life by doing things that would cause him to pay attention. One time, while my mom was having some type of girly-type party, I let the air out of all of my mom's friends' tires. When her guests tried to leave, my mom called my father and he had to come pump air in all their tires. That was one of many times I heard my mom say, "When your father gets home, you're going to get a spanking."

That was back when my parents were still together. My father never quit drinking until he was in his eighties. He was always getting in trouble, even while in the Air Force. Like father, like son in that respect. Back then, if you had a high rank in the military, people would cover for you. Back in the States, however, he'd go to work, drink, smoke, and raise hell without anyone being there to bail him out. One day, when I was thirteen years old, the trouble he got into couldn't be covered up anymore, so he left. He got into a hit and run accident and ran from the law until he reached Chicago. He stayed out of Washington State for seven years—until the warrant for his arrest expired. When he did return, my mom tracked him down, divorced him, and made sure he paid child support.

After my dad left, Mom went back to work after having been a stay-at-home mom, and my brother, by then eighteen, became the man of the house. I didn't get much discipline from him, though. He was more my protector. My brother, known as "Blair," was very popular. He was a football star; he dated all the cheerleaders and everybody grouped around him, often coming over to our house to work on cars. He was the nice kid, while I—"Little Blair"—was the little rascal. Nobody at school messed with me though, because if they messed with Little Blair, they'd have to mess with Blair. I had this bodyguard umbrella over me wherever I went. I felt bulletproof.

Then my mom remarried, and our stepfather thought he could discipline me. That didn't go over very well. My stepbrother even tried to show me who was boss—with a knife. By that time, I was active in sports and had become a pretty decent wrestler. Back before guns became popular, we used to do hand-to-hand combat if we wanted to beat people up. Well, this kid wanted to stab me, probably just for existing. Who knows what his mental issues were at the time. His father came home at the very moment when I jumped on him to take away the knife and thought I was attacking his kid, who was bigger than me. Then he realized that I wasn't trying to kill him, I was just defending myself.

In any case, we never did become one big, happy family. By the time I reached high school, he and my mom had divorced. My older brother caught him cheating on my mom, so that was the end of that.

I don't know that I missed my biological dad those years. He hadn't been that pleasant to be around. But I kept on trying to fill the void he left behind. I had a lot of different girlfriends over the years, and I would charm my way into their families. I was like Eddie Haskell in *Leave it to Beaver*, saying "Mrs. Cleaver, you look very nice today," while sneaking through their daughter's window.

But years down the road, when I was twenty-four or twenty-five years old, I'd made peace with my old man in my heart and wanted him back in my life. The trouble was he had never shown any interest in coming back. I knew I'd have to trick him. I called him up one day and told him that my brother had died and he needed to come back for the funeral. When I picked him up at the airport, he wanted to know the details. "Well, how did he die?" he asked. I said, "He didn't die, Dad. I just wanted you to come back."

That lie was one of the best lies I've told in my life. It

brought Dad back. I had a house on Spanaway Lake, south of Tacoma, and he came and stayed with me there for a week. Then he decided that he liked it there. I said, "Dad, come back. I need you back in my life because you've been gone." He moved everything that he had and came and lived with me. He stayed there until he met a woman at a bar, remarried and bought a house in Rochester, Washington. He lived to be eighty-eight years old.

What I got out of that bad upbringing was my commitment to never leave my children, never cheat on my wife, never be an alcoholic and never smoke. Dad left his mark on me in another way, too. Before he ran from the law, creating a trail of mess behind him, he was a master woods craftsman. He could make furniture and all sorts of cool stuff. His best friend and neighbor, Bud, was an ironworker and he owned a junkyard. Between his welding experience and my dad's wood craftsmen skills; they built a tiny home on a trailer. I believe they intended to take it hunting, though I don't know that they ever did. I am sure it lacked some basic amenities, but it was nevertheless a tiny home, before the "tiny home" buzz words existed.

Chapter 3:
Money Mindset

A special buddy and I went to school together from third grade through high school. Some of my earliest memories of him involve riding bikes. We both had Stingray bicycles and if we wanted to be really cool, we had to be able to ride on one wheel. We would practice yanking up the handlebars and balancing on one wheel to pull off the feat.

We lived only a few blocks from each other and we had about a five-block area that we'd ride through to get to a field where boys could be boys. Without adults around, we could talk about things boys talk about—which by age twelve or so, was sex. I didn't know what sex was until he told me. He said, "Did you know that you have to put you're ... in her ...?" And I went, "What? Really? That's how that works? No way." We joke about that to this day.

As we evolved into junior high school, we joined the wrestling team. He already had practiced with the sport from sparring with his older brother, who later became a golden glove champion boxer in the military. In high school, my buddy was a couple of weight groups ahead of me, so we didn't spar together on the team, but we did on our own and with other neighborhood kids. The trouble was, if someone wanted to pick a fight with us and looked at me and looked at him, they were going to pick on me. He picked on me sometimes, too, but always with good intention.

I already felt tough, but I credit his brother for making me tougher. I used to spar with him in his garage; we'd put on boxing gloves and he'd encourage me to give it my best shot to try to knock him out. I'd aim to the right, then the left, right, left, until finally—boom! I got him. I saw that look on his face that said, "Good, you've got it. Now I'll show you how it's really done." I was thinking, *Oh no, he's going to get me back.* And he did. He knocked me through their garage door and the garage door fell to the ground. His wife came out to find me in the middle of the flattened door, completely laid out, and said - "Why did you do that to Ronnie?" He simply answered, "He was just tagged by one of the best." It wasn't to be mean. He just wanted to show me the rules of the game.

We used to run together as well; we were both in cross country. We ran to get in shape for wrestling, which was the next season. When I was in trouble at home, I would use running as an excuse to get out of the house. I always got permission to leave because I had to run—it was a sports thing. It was school-related. Then I would run to the parties, I'd run to my girlfriend's house, I'd run and get homework that I had various girls doing for me. I never did my own homework. I was smart; I just couldn't prove it on paper.

So, my buddy and I went through sports, girls and coming of age together. We always had the fastest cars and the most adventure. We loved living on the edge. He would later get me involved with RVs.

I was eighteen years old and staying at a resort called Clearwood in Yelm, Washington. My girlfriend's parents owned a condo there, where we decided to throw a party one weekend. The morning after the party, I went outside and headed to my car. I came around the corner of the property, which was a duplex and that's where my path crossed with the man who would get me into real estate.

"Hi, I'm Lou, the man said." He was quite flamboyant, with a big collar sticking out, a gold chain, rings and things. I call it the Mr. T starter kit.

"Hi, I'm Ron Blair." I was curious to know who he was, and apparently, he was curious about me too. He said, "So, do you know Judd?" Judd was my girlfriend's dad. "Yeah, they invited me over and we partied last night. Now I'm headed home." "So, what do you do?" Lou asked."I work for Tacoma Screw Products." "What do you do there?" "I package the screws that you buy at Ace Hardware. What do you do?" "I've got sixty people that are smarter than me, working for me."

"Okay, but that doesn't tell me what you do, what do you do?" "I'm involved in marketing the property out here. All these lots are for sale." I said, "Oh really? Well, sell me a lot."

He said, "All right, jump in my car." He had this big

Oldsmobile that seemed like it could fit twenty people. It was a big old boat car that he would use for touring. Back then, I smoked weed, so I lit up a joint. He looked at me kind of funny, but I didn't care. We drove around in his car and he proceeded to give me his presentation. An hour later, I was buying a piece of property. I had no intention to buy before that and - no money.

He offered me a "no money plan," which meant that if I could afford $72.43 a month for the payment on that property, I could own the property. I just had to make six payments that went toward the down payment before I could get a key to the kingdom. The key was a card. You insert it in a machine and the gates opened up—and not just the gates to the property. I knew that if I could get into the property, there would be somebody in that kingdom I would meet that would make things change for me. I could smell the money inside those gates.

Clearwood is a very exclusive resort built by Quadrant Weyerhaeuser. It had 4,000 sites, all part of this gated community. There was a back gate and a front gate, a big clubhouse and various beach areas. Around three-quarters of Clear Lake belonged to the resort. The other quarter belonged to a smaller private resort and a few residential homes.

My lot was 50x100 feet—little postage stamp spot. As we were touring around, I could have picked any lot, but he offered me the cheapest one because he knew I had no money. Each of the lots came with power, water, septic hookups and was thickly wooded. He pushed this one lot on me that had a little private alley in the back. He envisioned for me, "What you could do is trim these trees up and make a little park-like setting."

I bought into everything he was saying. I signed up that day and paid my first six payments as scheduled and couldn't wait to get my card key and start building my little dream. I arrived at the resort's office, walked in, and saw Lou.

"Ronnie, how you doing?" he said. "I'm doing good", I replied. "You still working for Tacoma Screw Products?" he asked. "No, they screwed me", I confessed.

"What happened?" I told him the story about getting my welding certificate and coming back to find my last paycheck ready for me. They fired me because they wanted me to be a company man and my continued education had revealed my aim to improve myself with a new skill set.

Lou said, "Well, if you got screwed at Tacoma Screw, why don't you come sell real estate?" I said, "All right."

"It's going to require you to get a real estate license," he informed me. I was so naive I didn't care. So, I went and got a license. Back then you could get a temporary permit for six months to sell real estate. Immediately, he gave me a little packet and showed me where Lake Lucinda was, which was to be my first project in Washington State.

He said, "All I want you to do is go tell somebody that you're doing this and I'll meet you at the resort this weekend." I went and told one of my friends that was recently back from the service and had just gotten married, "I'm getting my real estate license and I'm selling … "

And lo and behold, one of my acquaintance, replied, "We're thinking about buying some property." I said, "Really? I don't know anything about this yet, but here is the property." I showed him the map and brochure I had just received from Lou. "That looks nice," he said.

"You can meet me there this weekend and be my first visitor." "Okay," he replied.

I showed him and his wife through the property and they ended up buying a lot. Beginner's luck, as they would say in real estate. But it wasn't beginner's luck. Anybody I brought down there would buy because I would introduce them to Lou, who knew what to do. I was the tour guy, but Lou was the closer.

I started bringing people in to see the property, not even knowing how to sell. However, I knew how to give tours. I would say, "Hypothetically, if you were going to buy one, would you want to be on the lake? Or would you want to be by the creek? Or somewhere without water?" They'd say, "Well, I don't know, maybe the lake."

I'd say, "Okay, let's go look at the lake lots." It was what is called the "if hypothesis," which is what Lou taught me to do: "Get them in the 'if'," he'd say, "because 'if' means it doesn't really happen unless they want it to." I would tell people on my tours, "If you were to do this, which one would you want?" and they'd say, "Well, if we were, we would pick that one." And that would create the fantasy of living on that lot.

Then I would say, "Ok, well, this one here is really cool because ..." Then I would say the same thing Lou told me: "You can trim up the trees and create a little park-like setting until you're ready to build." That's how I learned to give tours. My problem was the close. Nothing happens unless you can close the deal.

Lou said, "Don't worry about it, it will come to you. I know you can do it. You're just having a mental block." He started training me. He said, "I want you to do exactly what I say. Don't question anything. Memorize it. Do it. Think it. Ink it. Repeat it. Practice, drill and rehearse it. And I guarantee you if you do this, you'll be better than I am." At that point, I felt like I was listening to the God of Real Estate and God was saying if I do this, I'd be better than God. I thought if I could just do half of what he does I'd be so happy.

So, I did what he asked me to do. He asked me to listen to Zig Ziglar and Earl Nightingale and many other professional speakers. Back then we had cassette tapes and I played them so much that after a while I started to understand what they were saying. Earl Nightingale has such a deep, interesting voice that he'd put me in a trance just listening to him. And this is what I learned: You become what you think about.

Whatever you want to do, involve all of your senses—visualize it, write it out, say it out loud, rinse and repeat. Make your goal the first thing you think about in the morning, the last thing you think about before going to bed and the center of your thoughts all day. Create affirmations or positive-structured statements describing how you know you can be and repeat them to yourself. If anything tries to get in your way, dodge away from that; negative thoughts and people are what I call "deal killers." If you can manage to do all that, eventually, your thoughts will become real.

I went to seminars to reinforce those teachings; instead of walking away with a few takeaways, I took everything with me. I bought all the tapes and incorporated everything they said into my vocabulary. I was a brainwashed robot, but I was not in a cult or being misled. I saw the light and I used all of those tools to my advantage. And that's what turned me into a sales and marketing force to be reckoned with. This technique can be used to con people for bad or help people for good. And I chose the good side. I became the best student and rose to the top.

Then, off to the races I went. I sold out the rest of Lake Lucinda. Lou told me, "You just didn't see it before. Now you see it." There was a race among project managers at the time that whoever could sell out Lake Lucinda before Clearwood was sold out would get the next big project up on Whidbey Island, called Lagoon Point. It was waterfront property. Each property had a dock that went up and down with the tide and a private barge area. You can no longer build docks on the saltwater, but you could then. I was given this property to sell, and to my great fortune, it was underpriced; they didn't have accurate comparables.

Each property for sale included two lots that shared a T-shaped dock; the dock went down the property line and then turned right to one property's boat and left to the other's boat. But when I would show those two lots, I showed it as one piece of property. Since it was underpriced, I doubled the price because it was two lots. Then, when we'd go to close on the deal, right after viewing the property, I would tell them that for their benefit, their one lot had already been subdivided into two, so if they were to decide that one dock was more than they needed and they wanted to sell the other half, they didn't need to divide the property—it had already been done ahead for them.

So, people bought two lots, thinking it was just one. I sold two to four lots at a time. I was given two and a half years to sell out Lagoon Point. I sold it out in nineteen working days (working only weekends).

Lou's boss and managers had insulted him for hiring an eighteen-year-old to sell real estate. They said no one would listen to me, and I had no credibility. Of course, I didn't get that memo, and Lou didn't tell me that until after an awards banquet where I was honored for breaking a twelve-year-old sales record.

Then, all the managers that were eating crow at the awards banquet went to Lou and said, "Hey, does he have time to talk to my kid?" So, I began tutoring upper management's children, who were my age that grew up with golden spoons in their mouths and hadn't yet amounted to much.

What I learned about tutoring is that you have to create a vacuum. You can't just preach to kids. You have to use reverse psychology to lure them in. It's almost like being in a cult; cult people will not invite people close to them to join the cult if they don't already believe in the cult. An outsider has to be brought in. Kids won't listen to their parents, but if somebody else presents the same idea as their parents, they'll listen to a total stranger. I was that stranger. Since I was their same age, I was able to talk their language.

I gave them my story and then I would say, "People don't plan to be failures; they just fail to make plans." Then I'd ask, "What's your definition of success?" They would list money, a boat, and other things. I would explain that those are the fruits of success, but not the definition of success. I told them that success is the progressive realization of a predetermined, worthy goal.

It made a real impact on these kids. I was able to get their attention. I never did any follow up to see where their lives led though, because I was moving forward so fast in my own career.

Everything I touched was turning to gold.

The irony is, after I bought my Clearwood property and camped there a few times, I never really went back. Instead, I rented a house and then talked my friend into moving out of his parents' house and in with me. He was running his Uncle's successful RV dealership at the time. When I was selling real estate, he'd wake me up in the morning—I had a waterbed back then and he would put his foot on the bed, shake it and say, "Get up, you've got to come to work." I said, "I only work on the weekends - man." He'd say, "You need to come sell RVs. You can't just work two days a week." I was making $10,000 a month working two days a week, so yes—I could.

But after I sold out Lagoon Point, I essentially put myself out of business. Weyerhaeuser couldn't bring on another project for our team in that short amount of time because they had to get the property, develop the property, get it set up for sale, put in all the plumbing, water, and roads and all that. So, one morning, my buddy woke me up and said, "Now you *have* to come and work for me." And I did.

Chapter 4:
The Wild West

I could have gone into residential real estate or even commercial. I had my license, so I was set. But no—I chose to work with my buddy in the RV business. It wasn't just that it was convenient; I did try selling a residential property first, but after it took the standard ninety days to close—and therefore get paid—it made a lot more sense to sell RVs and earn a much quicker buck.

When I came in to work with my buddy, I was already the top agent for Quadrant Weyerhaeuser; I had been trained on how to handle sales transactions legally and professionally. I wore a three-piece suit, looking like a million dollars and hoping to make my first million. I represented what was good, fair, and honest. He had brought me into an industry that wasn't any of those things. It was the Wild, Wild West.

We had knives and guns and chains and alcoholics and drug addicts. That was my new theater of opportunity. Alcoholics had been in the industry for decades, but the new blood coming in were drug addicts. I didn't do either; once I got into real estate, I was straight as an arrow. I was stuck in the middle, like a referee between the drug addicts and the alcoholics. It was the perfect riptide. It wasn't like that across the industry; from the stories that I hear, other dealerships were wild, but we were the wildest.

I quickly became the top salesman; two years later I became the sales manager, and four years after that I became a general manager. Then, after eight years, I became one of the owners. We were the top RV dealership on the West coast.

Every day at the dealership, the same characters would show up. It was like an Etch a Sketch; they would shake it up and start over each day with only a vague memory of how intoxicated they were the day before. Everybody had their specialty drink. There was the Budweiser guy and there was the Mac with a water back guy.

When we'd show RVs, we would open up a cabinet and it would be loaded with booze. Or, we would flush the toilet and hear this little rattle. We'd lift the toilet lid and there would be vodka in there—one guy liked to keep his vodka on ice. Another guy just kept a cooler in his car. On the drug addict side of things, we had Cocaine Ken and LSD Larry, Smoke Weed Willy, and so forth.

Back then, there were no rules in sales. Showing up intoxicated or high to work - it was fine, as long as you made a sale. In fact, when we'd had sober sales people, these guys couldn't sell. They weren't aggressive enough. Drinking turned the "nice" filter off. It worked to my advantage, however, to stay sober. The strategy, which we all lived by, was to create chaos. If someone got too drunk or too high, he couldn't help a customer—which meant someone else got the sale. When everyone else was stirred up in a fight, we'd walk away and take their customer. In our business, we stopped at nothing in getting the sale.

Take, for instance, the time I was about to make a sale at our nearby location. I lived and worked near there, but the dealership's main branch was an hour drive away. Now, the particular RV model, that my customer wanted to buy, the Sahara, but they needed to test drive it first. So, I needed to get a ride up to main location and drive the Sahara back to my location so the customer could test drive it there the next morning.

So, I got my roommate to take me to the main location and drop me off and then he promptly took off. I saw the Sahara on the lot and set about getting into the RV and backing it out of the slot. That's when the Mac with a water back guy (who was, naturally, drunk at the time), started cursing at me, "Where are you going with that SOLD son of a bitch?" He had customers right behind him, who had just bought that particular RV. I said politely and professional said "Sir", I'm just going to get this serviced for your client." He said, "Don't give me that bullshit, give me those keys or I'm going to knock you on your ass."

I was a little embarrassed, because his customers were right there, watching him bodyguard their new motorhome. I gave him the keys and figured we'd talk it out after the customers left since it was way past closing time and the RV really did need to be serviced the next day before his buyers picked it up. Well, his attitude didn't change. He refused to give me the keys. So, now I was stuck at our main dealership, with no ride home. He offered for me to spend the night at his house. Despite a gut instinct that told me differently, I thought that agreeing to his offer would give me time to talk some sense into him and get the keys to the RV back.

We left the dealership, got into his vehicle and began driving down the road toward his home. There was a lot of traffic, however, so he started driving up over the sidewalks. I said, "Stop you're going to get pulled over." He said, "That's okay, I've already got twenty-six DWIs. I can get another one, don't matter to me." Somehow, he never got his driver's license taken away. Different times, I guess.

Before long, he started pulling off the road into a parking lot. "Where are we going," I asked. "We're stopping here for a nightcap," he replied. I thought, *well, that's just what we need, a nightcap. I just need the keys!* We went into the bar, with him dressed in his two-piece suit. He always looked sharp, despite always being drunk. He said to the bartender, "Give me a Mac with a water back and fix up the dummy with one, too." I was the dummy.

He downed his drink and then chased it with water. When he went back to take the shot, I reached over into his left pocket. There were no keys in it. I said, "Excuse me for a minute; I'm going to use the men's room." I came back and sat on his other side. As he went back to take his next shot, I looked into his right pocket. I thought, *Shit, they were not in the obvious place. He's probably got them in one of his other pockets.*

Finally, it was time to go. I told him he'd been drinking way too much, so he should let me drive. As we were driving, I mentioned that the mirror was a little wobbly. He grabbed the mirror, ripped it off the foundation, and threw it on the freeway. "That oughtta take care of that wiggly son of a bitch," he said. I guess it did.

We eventually got to his house, and his wife was standing on the porch—no doubt, like she did every day, waiting for him to get home. "Why did you bring Ronny here?" she asked. "He was drinking too much, so I thought I'd bring him home," he said. She then pointed out that I was driving not him.

He said, "Well, I've been drinking a little bit too, baby. Just put Ronny on the couch, he'll be good for the night." We went inside, she gave me a blanket and a pillow, and I got settled on the couch. In less than five minutes, the lights went out and they went to bed. I was still thinking *I have to get those keys.*

So, I walked through the dark house, down the dark hallway, and I saw their bedroom door cracked a bit. I got down on my hands and knees and crawled around their bedroom floor, looking for the keys to the motorhome. Then I saw a glow on the floor. *What is that? A glowworm?* I thought. It was one of his cigarettes that had fallen from the ashtray on his nightstand onto the carpet and was starting to smolder on the floor. I picked it up, put it in my mouth, and used it as a little flashlight. When I puffed on it, it would glow.

At the foot of the nightstand, I saw the keys. *How lucky is that*, I thought! I got the keys and was so excited I got up and knocked something over. His wife woke up and said, "There's someone in the room!" And of course, he had guns everywhere, so I was thinking I was going to get shot. I ran through their master bedroom, into the master bathroom, opened the window and jumped through, landing in their backyard. I'd never been to his house before, but I knew I needed to get to my destination.

Until that point, I'd never been in a taxi that I had to pay for. I had only twenty dollars on me, so I found a phone booth on the nearest corner, called a cab and told him where I was and where I needed to go, then asked how much it would cost. He said about fifteen dollars, so I said okay. The driver came and picked me up and we were driving down the highway, when the meter hit fifteen dollars. I thought, *Oh no, I've only got twenty dollars and we're not even halfway there yet. What am I going to do?!*

Instead of going into the dealership, I asked him to drop me off at the dealership next door, which was our neighbor that sold Winnebago's. I said, "Sometimes these motor homes don't start, so just wait right here for me, I might need a ride further." I walked a couple of motor homes down and said, "It's this one here, I'll be right back, I have to try and start it." I ran in between motor homes and out of sight, then jumped the fence over into our dealership, got the motorhome and drove away.

I had gotten almost home when I ran out of gas. I hadn't even thought about gas, my adrenaline was pumping so hard from escaping the taxi I couldn't pay for, in his motor home that he'd just sold, while his wife was wondering who broke into their house. I pulled over to the side of the road and called for another cab. I still had twenty bucks.

I'm certainly not proud of this fact now, but as a nineteen-year-old wheeler and dealer, I thought, *hey, this is great! I can ride taxis without having to pay if I do it right.* I got three houses from where I lived and said, "Here's my house, right here." The driver pulled into the neighbor's driveway, who I didn't even know, and I got out of the car and went to the front door. I acted like it was my home and it was locked, so I gave him the signal that I was going around to the back. I went around to the back and jumped the fence and a dog started chasing me through the backyard. I ran down the alley, trying to save my life from the dog I didn't even know lived there, but finally reached my house. I got inside, looked out the window and saw the cab driver honking his horn and flashing his lights - then eventually driving away.

I got my roommate to drive me back to the motorhome after stopping to fill up a gas can. When we arrived, I saw someone had broken the window. I got the RV back to the dealership, however and ready to be test-driven the next morning. I made the sale, telling them that they couldn't have this particular RV because the window was broken, so they'd have to wait for a duplicate to be brought in. I then brought the motor home back to the main dealership.

"You deliberately sabotaged my deal!" He said. "You broke the window!"

I said, "No, that's not what happened." I explained the previous day to him, because he didn't remember any of it, and perhaps twisted facts a bit.

In the Wild West, you do whatever it takes to make the deal. You also do whatever it takes to protect yourself. My life was threatened on an almost daily basis working with those guys.

Here's a quick story from the showroom floor that I'll never forget. One day, one of the guys thought I had sold an RV to one of his customers, which would have meant I'd get the commission. He went to look for the paperwork, but instead of finding paperwork for his client, he found my paperwork for another RV that I sold that day. Perhaps out of disappointment at busting me, he wadded the paperwork up and threw it in the garbage can, where I found it later that day.

I approached him about it and said, "Hey, you threw my paperwork away? That's totally unacceptable!" He got off the couch he normally slept on because he was drunk all the time, went to the coffeemaker, poured himself a cup and I got the sense he was going to throw it at me. As suspected, he threw the coffee at me, but I was ready for it. I spun around, missing the coffee flying in the air, did a roundhouse kick and hit him in the head. He fell down, right next to an iron rod that we'd use to pull awnings down on motorhomes. He reached for the rod, which I knew he was going to swing at me, so I took it away from him and backed off.

One of the owners yelled at the trouble maker to knock it off. He responded by getting out his knife, which he proceeded to swing at me. Our fight moved to another section of the showroom floor, where a chain was lying on the floor. I thought, *either I pick that up or he's going to pick it up.* I second-guessed myself, thinking, *no, he won't pick it up,* which was of course a mistake. He picked it up and started swinging the chain at me, like an expert cowboy with his lasso, in the parts department of the store, with customers everywhere. This was happening in one of the largest dealerships on the west coast—and it wasn't even an unusual day. Eventually, I managed to get out to my car and drive away. He was escorted out and didn't come back for thirty days.

For thirteen years, while working at the dealership, that was just another day on the job. And, that was just the sales department—the service department was a wild bunch, too. Most of those guys have since passed away. People don't last long, living that lifestyle. But somehow, a couple of them are still alive, still a drunk and still crazy. I later introduced one of the guys into real estate, which made for a cleaner life. He made millions of dollars, retired and became quite spiritual. But he's still got a little bit of that old wild side in him.

And, as the propane burns, so do the days of our lives.

Chapter 5:
Losing Religion

When I met my first wife, my friend and I were down in Olympia, driving around in his 1966 Bentley. It was tan colored with a brown, wavy stripe and a sunroof. It was gorgeous and probably contributed to the confidence I felt as we rolled into the parking lot of a local night club.

We parked the car and went inside to meet a couple of his friends. While he went to greet them at the bar, I started checking out the inventory. To my pleasure, I saw two blondes sitting alone at a table. I thought *they need to be dancing.* I told the guys I was going to ask them for a dance and strolled on over to the smokin' hot one. Well, she denied me. Now, any guy knows you can't just walk away after getting denied—not in front of your friends. So, I turned to the next girl, who had just been in a car accident. Her face was bruised and both eyes were black and blue.

"Would you like to dance?" I asked.

She said, "I can barely walk."

"That's okay. I'll be easy on you," I replied, with my game face on. We got up, did a little dance and the next thing we knew, the bar was closing.

"Do you guys want to have breakfast?" The ladies asked us. He and I met up with the ladies at an all-night diner, where I started rubbing Blondie's shoulders because she'd been wounded. I've got healing fingers. She melted.

After breakfast, he and I were perfect gentlemen; we jumped in the Bentley and drove back to home. Blondie had given me her number and told me where she worked. She was the main bartender at a western bar. I drove down there a few days later and saw her running the bar. Her face had healed somewhat since we'd met and I saw how hot she was, as she made drinks faster than Tom Cruise in the movie *Cocktails*. She would break glasses while the bar backs swept up the glass behind her. There were men hitting on her, but I thought I probably had a better chance than anyone else there. I asked her out, and we started dating. She had a lot of endearing qualities; she was beautiful, a pianist, and an amazing singer. Before long, we were talking about getting married. What a mistake that was. Don't pick up girls in a bar, because you might marry them.

While we were dating, she told me she wanted to be a Jehovah's Witness but hadn't been baptized yet. I thought, *Jehovah's Witness?! There's something wrong with those people.* They were like Kirby vacuum cleaner salespeople, coming to your door and preaching the Bible. To be fair, I didn't know much about the religion, but I was Christian, so I told her, "Well, if we're going to get married, I'm either going to be a Jehovah's Witness or you're not." It's like a marriage between a Democrat and a Republican; how do you keep them in the same household?

Jehovah's Witnesses, I found out, were quite a challenge. A friend of mine was an ordained minister. I asked him, "Do you know anything about these Jehovah's Witnesses?"

"Oh, boy, do I. I did my thesis on Jehovah's Witnesses," he said. "I'll tell you a couple of things. If you're going to have a meeting with them, there's a question you need to ask." He explained how Jehovah's Witnesses like to have an initial get together with new recruits to start their brainwashing. He told me to ask about John 1:1 in their Bible, where the capital "G" in God is changed to a little "g." Their thought was that they don't believe Jesus was God, so they took away His authority by making him another god—in the same way Satan is a god. But the problem with that logic is that Revelations says that if any man alters or adds to the word of God in this book, God would respond by adding unto him a plague—or some form of punishment.

So, I dressed up in a suit and went to one of the Jehovah's Witness Kingdom Halls. (They don't call their places of worship "churches," because those are pagan.) I sat in the front pew. They asked, "Is anyone here new?" I raised my hand. "Welcome," they said. "Do you have any questions for us?" I replied, "Yes, I'm not real familiar with how this works, but I've always been curious about John 1:1, which says that in the beginning was the Word and the Word was God. You guys changed God to a small 'g,' which throws off the book of Revelations. How do you explain that?" They did not quite know how to deal with me, because no one was brave enough to ask that question. I was escorted away, and my address was permanently marked as a door not to be knocked on.

I was determined, however, to get my soon-to-be-wife, whom I loved, to see the light. I became very studious regarding how to deal with Jehovah's Witnesses. My friend became my mentor, but on the religious side. I became obsessed with studying the religion, to the point where I essentially locked myself in my office for four months, instead of making sales.

Finally, my boss said to me, "Ron, if you're going to come to work, you need to work. You need to dump this girl. There's a lot of fish in the sea. You don't need that one. It's costing me a fortune." He was more worried about the money than my love for this girl.

I decided to take a six-month sabbatical. I had enough money to get by without working for a while. I became an authority on Jehovah's Witnesses. Since I'm a marketing guy, I set up my own 24-hour answering service. I put ads in the Little Nickel, a Jehovah's Witness 24-hour watch line, for people to call with questions about the religion. I lured Jehovah's Witnesses in under the premise that I would answer questions about their faith, but in the end, I helped forty-two of them accept Jesus.

I got my girlfriend to accept Jesus with the same principles I used on the hotline. Romans 10:9, "If you believe in your heart and confess with your mouth that Jesus is Lord, you will be saved." But Jehovah's Witnesses don't believe you'll be saved. You have to work for it. And you might be one of the 144,000 that get to go to Heaven, but the rest are left behind.

When my fiancé read Romans 10:9, the Holy Spirit zapped her. She fell back and started talking in tongues, which Jehovah's Witnesses don't believe in. She instantly went from being a Jehovah's Witness to a Christian talking in tongues. I'd heard about people speaking in tongues, but I'd never seen anyone do it. I took her to the hospital because I thought she was having a breakdown. The doctor's diagnosis was: "She had a religious experience, we see this happen from time to time." It was just another day at the office for medical personnel.

After that, my fiancé had to go through a deprogramming (i.e. if that's a lie, then what else was a lie?) and figure out what the truths of what she'd been taught were, because Jehovah's Witnesses take some parts from the Bible and twist the rest. But—she was converted. My job was done.

I went back to the office the next day. My boss was glad I was back. The rest of my RV career continued, and Blondie and I got married. But the marriage didn't last. It turns out, she was an alcoholic. Who would have thought? She stayed at home all day, drank, and read the Bible. When I got home she'd be drunk, but for a long time I couldn't tell—she hid it very well. The habit had formed years before, back when she was a practicing Jehovah's Witness.

I was at a big Jehovah's Witness convention once at a revival. I talked to the liquor control guy in that zip code and he said that every year at that convention, they run out of liquor. Liquor is frowned upon in the religion. When something is forbidden, everybody wants it. I may have gotten Blondie to lose her religion, but the damage had already been done. After seven years, no kids, and one Doberman, I left. I kept my religion—and the Doberman.

Chapter 6:
The Fixer

In 1988, I opened my own facility. I was ready for new horizons—my own business and apparently a new wife. After selling several RVs to a government official, he suggested I open up my own dealership in a particular market area. That was the birth of my first dealership.

After experiencing firsthand the Wild West culture of the RV industry, I did all of the hiring myself. With the advent of the internet and the abundance of information readily available to consumers, buyers were becoming more educated and sellers had to get sharper.

The business was a success, and it probably showed in the way I dressed and the cars I drove. You'd think I would have learned my lesson about not meeting future wives in bars, but I did not. I have a record of attracting broken people who I think I can fix. In this case, I'm the one who got played.

One day after work, I strolled into a bar dressed in a three-piece suit that made me look like a million bucks. It was happy hour, where one hour would typically slide into the next hour and the next. As usual, I became distracted by a couple of hot girls at the bar. One of the wholesalers

I knew—who I called the godfather of the gypsies since he was in the upper echelon of the community—was over there talking to them, also dressed in a suit and looking confident.

The problem was, he was not their type. I figured he had no chance with women that hot, so I walked up to him and said, "Hey dude, you know these girls are high quality. And you? You look good in a suit, but you're not the right guy. I'll take it from here." I pushed him aside. It was bold and brass and I guess the girls liked it. He bowed out with no resistance, moving on to the next group of girls.

One woman in particular responded to my bravado. She must have smelled money, even though I was sniffin' for love. She had these gorgeous bedroom eyes and hair so thick it made me forget all logic and reason. Within six months, we were married. The other woman at the bar was the bridesmaid in our wedding.

Meanwhile, business kept growing and my dealership became the top Interstate battery retailer for the peninsula in the county because I sold so many RVs. Every RV takes two batteries, so I sold around 300 batteries a month just by selling RVs. Business boomed at my first RV show, I sold fifty-five RVs in five days. I called my wife, who was a bank teller and told her, "Baby, you need to resign from the bank because we're making too much money - I can't keep track of all the invoices and payables - come count our money instead of the banks" - so she did.

Within thirty days of working for me, she was so

stressed out trying to keep track of all the sales herself, that she told me I needed to stop selling. The factory rep heard this, pulled my wife aside and said, "You either need to hire more people or replace yourself, because in this business, you don't ask someone to stop selling." That was an eye-opener for her. She probably thought - wait, I can leave him sooner if I get more help and he keeps selling. I learned that in retrospect.

After three years of marriage, the battery wholesaler who, of course, was coming around often—came around for the last time. He would come to the office and tell me how many batteries were sold and I'd authorize my wife to write him a check and she'd give it to him. That wasn't the only thing she was giving him, however, one of my employees tipped me off that she'd been seen getting busy with battery guy at a bar.

I did some investigating, and it turned out to be true. So, the next and last time he came in to get a check, I said, "Hang on a second, I've got to make a conference call." I called battery guy's wife and said, "Hi Lisa, I've got your husband here. He's got something he wants to tell you. He and my wife are having an affair." I caught him right on the spot.

About a year after our divorce (and after battery guy's marriage to my ex-wife), I ran into the bridesmaid from our wedding, who had been at the bar the night I'd met her. She said, "Hi. I don't know if you remember me, but I'm really sorry." "What'd you do?" I asked, not recognizing her. "I was the bridesmaid for your wedding." "Oh yeah, I remember you. But why are you sorry?"

"Well, the night you met your ex-wife at the bar, she told me it was where women went to pick up a guy that's got money. You marry him, divorce him and take their money and that's what happened to you."

"Are you kidding me?" I said, incredulous. I should have known. She got a multi-million -dollar divorce settlement out of me—half of everything for only three years of marriage. No kids, no dogs, not even a fish to split. Damn it - I should have let the wholesaler that was with me when I met her - have her.

No more picking up women in bars and keeping them, I told myself what I'd already told myself before. Do as I say, not as I do.

So that was wife number two. And then there was the third and final wife (I swore). She was the sister of one of the cousins who co-owned the previous dealership I worked for, that should already have been a red flag. Another lesson I should have learned - was to stay away from smokin' hot women.

She was only ninety-eight pounds, 4'11." She was Native American, with gorgeous, naturally dark brown hair. She was also bipolar, though I didn't even know that term or what it meant until we were going through a divorce and my lawyer subpoenaed her health records. I survived eight years of marriage to a beautiful, chemically imbalanced, maniacal woman. I won't go into the details of what that relationship was like, but I will say that, on the bright side, I got two beautiful daughters out of the union. They were the only reason the marriage lasted as long as it did. Rather than have me try to write about those years, I'll let my oldest daughter, Demi, share some of her memories in my last chapter.

After Demi was born, she wanted to have another child. She got pregnant again, but due to malpractice, she almost died. Sadly, the baby Blake Austin, did die. After that, we decided to adopt a second child. Adoption is a long and complicated process and the easiest route is to find someone you know who is pregnant and doesn't want to keep the baby. She told everyone she knew that we were looking to adopt. As it turned out, her sister had a co-worker with a fourteen-year-old stepdaughter who became pregnant and was either going to abort or adopt out. That baby became our daughter, De'Aunna.

She was able to go to all of the pre-baby appointments and when the baby was born, I was there to cut the umbilical cord. It was awkward because she made me video the birth, so there I was balancing a camera on my shoulder with my left hand and scissors in my right hand. I was too young to fully take in the gravity of the moment; I was just going through the motions at that point in my life. However, like Demi, De'Aunna became another great gift in my life.

I have many great memories of being with the girls. One of my favorites is when I took my mother, Demi and

De'Aunna to the beach in my nineteen-foot Airstream van. While we were hanging out at the beach one sunny day, De'Aunna, who was around four years old at the time, was sitting under an umbrella when the wind picked up. De'Aunna grabbed the umbrella, which was starting to fly away and got to have a Mary Poppins moment, suspended in midair.

Throughout their youth, we always did something fun on weekends. We'd go skating or snow tubing or skiing in the mountains. I remember when De'Aunna was only six years old, she'd put on skis and be gone—I'd have to run after her and catch her. She was a natural.

Both my girls became great artists. I've always loved to paint, so they may have gotten their artistic sides from me, but certainly not my style. I make mistakes in my artwork, but it's easy to cover up because my style is more like Picasso—it's unrealistic, anyway. Demi and De'Aunna however, are precise with their drawings; they'll use pencil or colored pencil and take hours or days to create their masterpieces.

Unlike my artwork, I couldn't "fix" my third wife, though I do like to believe I was a good father to our two children. It doesn't sound like a nice thing to say, but I did my best to protect them from their mother. They are two lovely adult women today; Demi is married to a great man who is the perfect complement to her. De'Aunna is happily married to a great guy as well and has a beautiful baby girl. That makes me Grandpa Ron; instead of trying to fix what is already perfect, my job is to teach that baby bad habits.

Chapter 7:
Mid-Century Milestones

Needless to say, life could be stressful at times. However, I didn't notice any red flags or consider how my lifestyle might cause strain on my health. I never got sick and very rarely went to a doctor. Regardless, reaching the fifty-year milestone made me pause long enough to make an appointment for a physical exam. It was 2007 - my kids were six and eleven years old and I wanted to stay healthy for them.

I went to my appointment and told the doctor I figured it was time for a check-up. He began examining my eyes, ears, nose and throat. When he got to my throat, he paused. "What's this?" he said, focusing his attention on a small lump. "Oh, it's just a swollen gland or something, I don't know - no big deal," I replied. "No, that's not a gland - it's something else and you need to have that checked out, he said". "Alright, I replied, what does that mean?"

He said, "It means we have to schedule you for a biopsy."

I thought, *I don't even know what a biopsy is. Now I'm going to get one.* I agonized over that for about two days while waiting for the appointment. I went in for the exam and this gorgeous, female doctor hooked me up to an ultrasound. While looking at the TV screen, showing the inside of my throat, she said, "Yeah, you've got something going on there and we're going to need to do the biopsy." I asked, "So, how does this work?" She said, "I just stick a needle down in there and pull a tissue sample out."

I would never have been a good drug addict because I can't handle needles at all. "A needle in my throat? I am so not doing that," I whined. "Well, you can agonize over it for a couple of weeks because that's how far we're booked out, or I could do it right now and you'll know tomorrow," she retaliated.

I figured I couldn't look like a weenie in front of this beautiful woman. So, in went the needle. I watched the whole thing go down, about ready to pass out, but then it didn't hurt at all. It was just the thought of it that freaked me out, and I didn't even feel it because they did local anesthesia around the area.

I went home, not expecting the worst. The doctor called me the next day and got right to the point: "I normally don't do this over the phone," she said, "but I'm leaving for vacation and you have cancer."

It was a June day, about eighty degrees outside. I was leaning against the side of my RV dealership looking into the sun. *Cancer? Who is this again? Is this happening to me?* My mind tried to make sense of what I was just told. *This kind of thing happens on TV or to the neighbor*, I thought, *but it doesn't happen to you. To me.*

The first call I made was to my mom. I told her the

news and that I needed to go in and have more tests done to determine what stage the cancer was in. Mom held her emotions together on the call but I imagine it was very hard news for her to hear. My older brother had died of cancer five years earlier.

After additional testing, I found out I had stage four throat cancer. I was given three months to live. I had stage four throat cancer and couldn't even feel it. If I wouldn't have gone in for a casual, fifty-year tune-up, I would never have known. I would have died, without any clues.

I was assigned an eye, ear, nose and throat doctor as my main doctor. I also had an oncologist and a radiologist. I had to go to an orientation before they could start treatment. As it turned out, when I was ready to begin, my doctor was out of town on vacation. As an alternative, I was led to the top oncology guy on the planet, who was based in Portland, Oregon. I only saw him once. "How long have you been smoking?" he started with. "I've never smoked a day in my life," I said. He said, "Do you want your mother to leave the room so you can tell me the truth?"

I was fifty years old and he was telling me my mother should leave the room so I could be honest. "My son has never smoked," my mom answered for me because I was speechless. The guy's bedside manners were terrible.

Then he said, "Well, treatment will be thirty-three radiations and three chemos over about two months, but it'll be a waste of time. You have no chance of making it three months, maybe six if you're lucky. You need to go get your affairs in order because there's no surviving this. You're stage four."

We left; my mom was sniffling and crying. I said, "Mom, don't worry about it. I'm firing that guy. He's gone. We'll never see that guy again."

I waited until my main doctor returned and went to see him. "Oh, don't listen to that guy," he said. "Things have changed. If you can survive the treatment, I guarantee that you'll die from something else. You'll never have a problem with throat cancer again."

I went through my series of prescribed treatments—starting with thirty-three radiation sessions. They radiated my throat and my tongue. As I'd been warned, I completely lost my taste buds, never to have them return in the same way as before. I also lost my saliva; I needed to have water with me at all times in order to swallow any type of food. "You'll eat to survive," the doctor had said. "You won't taste food, and it'll take you two years to recover."

I remember lying in the hospital bed, the words *two years* echoing in my head. "What do you mean, two years?" I asked. I thought, *Wow, I don't have two years scheduled not to work*. The doctor said, "Well, that's what the recovery time is." So, I sucked it up and moved forward with my treatment, trying not to think too much about the future of my career.

It was pretty brutalizing. Throat cancer treatment is

one of the hardest forms of cancer to recover from. Most people who die from throat cancer die from malnutrition. I was hospitalized three times because I couldn't get enough nutrition through the feeding pump. All food had to be liquid; it went to my stomach through a feeding tube. It was demoralizing to swing that contraption around with me everywhere I went. But you do what you have to do.

During my thirty-three radiations, I did my three chemos in a room with all these other people that were dying. Everyone was hooked up to IVs in beds. It would take all day to get the drugs through my system, then they'd let me go. The last one almost killed me; I don't think I was hydrated enough, and I got really sick. It was the most discomfort I'd ever been in. But I survived.

This was when all of the motivational experience I'd gained from my early real estate training kicked in. There was no way I was going to believe that first doctor who said I was going to die in three months. If I would have listened to him and believed him—the main authority in the industry, that most other people would believe—I probably would have gone home and gotten my affairs in order and died. You become what you think about. I was not thinking about dying. I was practicing positive thinking. I had a treatment plan; I was going to work through it and get to the other side.

After the treatment was all over, the doctors said, "You can't get your feeding tube out until you've eaten real food for thirty days. We don't want to have to put it back in again." I had to re-learn how to swallow. Thankfully, I discovered this magical organic stuff that's made in the Orient that's thick as molasses. It's like bottled syrup; I would mix it with hot water, like a tea, and put it in my mouth. It cleared up all the sores in my mouth from radiation within twenty-four hours. It was the first thing I was able to swallow.

After thirty days, I was ready to get my feeding tube taken out. When the tube was put in, I had needed to have an operation, but the doctor said I would not need to be cut open to have it taken out—it would just "pop right out."

I should have known it wouldn't be so simple. Having the tube was like having another belly button; this little ball was free-floating in my stomach, attached to the syringe and the tube. It was not sewn in. The doctor should have been able to just pull it out, as he'd said. So, I scheduled the appointment only two days before I was going to Mexico for vacation. I didn't want to trail that thing along with me to the beach.

I went to my appointment, which was not even day surgery. It was supposed to take ten minutes. The doctor was probably about 6'2"; he was a big guy. He put me on the bed, placed some towels around me and tried to pull the tube out.

He was moaning and groaning, and the tube was not budging. "It's not coming out," he said to me, dumbfounded. He put one foot up on the table to leverage himself while yanking on this thing inside of me, and I started screaming. It was like trying to pull a squid out of a marble hole, it was awful. The nurses came running in, "What's wrong?!" "I don't know what's going on," he said. "I've never had this happen before, but it won't come out. We're going to have to schedule surgery and cut it out."

"Uh, I'm leaving for Mexico in two days," I stared at him, my mouth agape. "I don't think we can get you in that soon," the doctor said. But he made a phone call and got me an appointment for the next day at a nearby clinic.

I went to the appointment and after the doctor introduced himself and attempted to pull the tube out, with similar results as the day before, he turned to me and said, "I'll be right back. I've got to get a couple of things." He went out but left the door open just a little bit. I could hear him say to the nurse, "I've got this. I don't need any help, but if you hear a scream, don't worry. I have to cut him."

Wtf?! He came back in, and I lashed out. "You're going to cut me?!" "You heard that?" "Yeah..."I said."It's okay," he said. "I'm going to put a local on it and you won't feel a thing."

Not really what I wanted to hear, but I had no choice. He gave me the anesthesia, cut away at my stomach, and pulled out the octopus-looking creature that was housed inside my body. "You want to keep this for a souvenir?" he asked. "No way. I never want to see that again in my life," I replied.

He threw it in the garbage, sewed me up, and I was done. The next day, I was in Mexico. My friend and I stayed at a resort, where I holed up and stuffed myself silly. I went to all the buffet meals I could. I didn't have a lot of energy; my immune system had been so compromised that I was perfectly content sitting on a lawn chair by the pool all day, only rising to go eat.

By this time, I had missed only about four weeks of work. If I went according to the doctor's prediction, I would miss two years. That didn't happen. I had a small RV dealership at the time that I'd started just before my diagnosis. I'd hired a salesman to run the place in my absence. After I returned from Mexico, my salesman called and said, "I've fallen and I can't get up."

I said, "I'm really not feeling up to playing any games right now." "No, seriously," he said. "I'm hobbled. The bone is sticking out of my foot. I slipped on the ice at the lot." "Okay, I'll be right down," I said. I showed up to the lot and sure enough, he was lying in the lot, hobbled. I helped him into my truck and took him to the hospital. It would not be a quick recovery; he broke his ankle sideways. He received the diagnosis and I thought, *Alright. I have to go back to work. There's nobody there. I'm the guy now.*

I was still in recovery myself, so I went in at 10 a.m. instead of 9 a.m. and left at 1 p.m. instead of 5 p.m. I gradually started coming in five minutes earlier and staying five minutes later, then ten minutes earlier and ten minutes later until I was back full speed in thirty days. I was the fastest recovery throat cancer patient in the history of Kaiser Permanente.

I attribute my recovery to mindset, and to having taken nutritional supplements every day, religiously. I also took CoQ10, fish oils, and Emergen-C twice a day. I got all my taste buds back within thirty days of completing treatment—now I like every food that I always hated before, in addition to all those I loved. I also attribute my recovery to my Mother, my hero.

Chapter 8:
Becoming the Tiny Home Guy

Surviving cancer was a major turning point in my life. Not only did it cause me to form healthier habits (i.e. eating better, not working so much and not marrying mad women). It opened my mind to exploring a new industry. Maybe I didn't want to be "the RV Guy" my whole life.

The small RV dealership I'd started just before the diagnosis was located on a gravel lot off of Highway 12 in Rochester, Washington. A few years later I moved the dealership to Interstate 5 at Exit 88, where it remains today.

About eight years ago, on a very busy June day, I saw a man walk into the office looking like a phone book salesman. My salesman addressed him. He didn't stay long, but long enough to leave behind a brochure, which my salesman plopped on my desk.

"This is supposed to be the latest, greatest thing. This guy's selling sheds," my rep said. I took a look at the brochure, which had a little business plan attached to it explaining what my costs would be, what the retail value was, etc.

"Why didn't you let me talk to this guy?" I asked. "We

sell RVs, not sheds," he replied. He had a point. But I was still intrigued. I got on the phone and called the guy. He picked up on the first ring.

"Are you still in the neighborhood?" I asked. "Yeah, I'm down at the next exit, I'm headed south to California and I'm just getting fuel", he replied. "Well, do you have time to come back? I'm available." "Yeah, I'll be right there," he replied. The guy was an importer-exporter. He had dual citizenship with Canada and Poland and could only be in the United States for a short time. He was selling these little garden sheds that looked more like the tiny homes of today. They were high-quality, wooden structures and the hook for me was that they were adorable. This guy was just trying to break into the shed business, looking for shed companies to take on another brand, but in my mind, I saw them as an aftermarket product. Nearly everyone that has an RV has a resort property somewhere that serves as a camping site. They would benefit from having a place there to store their barbecue, lawn chairs, and whatnot. To me, these adorable sheds were accessory items for my customers.

By then, the tiny home craze had already begun, but I was oblivious to it. I had been too focused on RVs and -well, fighting cancer. What I didn't see initially was that these sheds were, in essence, tiny homes -but that would come later.

The guy came, gave me his little presentation and turned to leave, saying, "Here's my card, give me a call if you're interested." I didn't need to think about it. I liked the idea of the sheds, they looked cute and it was a package deal. It was a do-it-yourself product and I saw that I could make money.

I said, "Now, wait a minute, has anyone bought these already?" "Not really, I just got here, he said". "I came in from Canada, working my way to California, but one guy in Oregon has placed an order." *Darn*, I thought, I wanted exclusive marketing rights for being the first retailer in North America.

"Where do these come from," I asked. "Well, they come from Europe on a ship and then they offload them at a port", he replied. Continuing my inquiry, "How do you get the sheds across to the United States -on a train?" "No, they go through the Panama Canal and up to the Pacific coast", he replied. "So, if I order some for Florida, I could beat the guy in Oregon, because it's faster?" I asked. "Yeah, you could," he said. BINGO, I thought to myself.

"Well, hang on a second." I called my buddy Norm in Florida and said, "Hey, can you let me store some products there?" Norm said, "No problem."

So, I bought two, forty-foot containers—one for Washington and one for Florida. One went to Florida while the second container went to Washington through the Panama Canal. So, Pasha (my builder guy) and I flew to Florida to get the "Tiny Homes" out of the containers they were shipped in. I had no idea how these were going to come out of a shipping container. I'd never bought anything that way before. We got a small forklift, which turned out to not be able to lift anything close to the size of the shipment. We needed an industrial-strength forklift. So, I had Pasha to take on the task—he's from Russia and Russians know how to do everything. He said, "No problem, boss man, we'll get a tow truck." He got the tow truck, backed it up to the container, hoisted them out with a winch and then forked them out. I would not have thought of that being the best way to handle the situation. I'm a marketing guy, not a forklift guy.

Because of my enthusiasm, the shed guy offered, "I think you should represent the United States." He knew I was a wholesaler with a dealer network all around the United States. So, I became the exclusive marketing agent for their company. I would set up dealers around the United States. I didn't want to be one of the guys selling them off the side of the road like pumpkins. I wanted to set everybody else up to sell them on the side of the road. I got my import-export license and became a broker. I immediately got licensed, bonded and insured.

I started setting up dealers all over the place. But in order to travel around and display the product, I had to put one on a trailer. I built my first one and attached it to the back of my truck. The tiny home kit was originally twelve feet in length and twelve feet wide, but I had to cut it down to eight-and-a-half feet to fit on the trailer. In this way, I got people all excited about them and dealers would buy them, but the problem would come once their order arrived. The dealers didn't know how to get them out of the containers. I had to be there when their orders arrived, to teach them how to do it. Then, once they had that figured out, they struggled with putting the kits together. The kits were supposed to be DIY, but these guys weren't always skilled with contractor/builder abilities. They were salespeople. But consumers want to see the finished product before they buy anything; you can't just show them a brochure.

It was very complicated and RV dealers want turnkey instant pudding. They want the RV to roll into the showroom and be able to say, "Ain't it pretty? Want to buy it?" So that was the end of that business venture. I'm sure some of those kits are sitting in RV lots, with termites taking care of them as we speak.

So, then I had to turn my marketing plan in a different direction. I already had a six-by-six tiny home, sitting on a trailer, looking like an RV. Why not sell it as an RV? It looked just like a tiny home because it was a tiny home—it unofficially held a Guinness World Record for the tiniest home on a trailer - a whopping thirty-six-square-feet of cuteness. As luck would have it, a woman from Vermont named Christina and her home-schooled daughter would end up moving in the same direction.

She was driving by my RV lot on her way to visit her mother near Woodinville, Washington when she saw my tiny home creation. She pulled over, got out and approached me. "I want to build a tiny home on a trailer!" she said.

"Well, I'll help you," I said. As you can see, "I've done a few here."

After shopping from East Coast to West Coast, they had the confidence to allow us to help her build her own tiny home. Even though we did 95% of the work, her 5% garnered her many photo opportunities. At that point, I had designed and built an eight-and-a-half-foot by twenty-foot tiny home on a trailer, like a Winnebago, that would assemble to interlock like Lego's and Lincoln Logs. All the pieces were pre-cut. The kit included the front, back and side walls to build the shell. Once the shell was up, you could decide where you'd want your bedroom, bathroom, kitchen, etc. I placed blue tape around the shell, showing where the stairs, walls and sink would go.

When Christina came to look at the models, what sold her on buying one was the fact that she wanted her daughter to have her own bedroom. All other models had only a one-bedroom loft. I figured out that the patio area could be enclosed, making another bedroom over the porch. They loved that idea. From that point on, all of my models had the extra bedroom for a bed or storage. I told Christina she could park her Airstream at my RV dealership and live there while her custom tiny home was built.

It turns out, Christina already had an agent for HGTV who was waiting for her to pick the tiny home she wanted, to be featured on the show *Tiny House Hunters*. Now, she'd found it. We called her agent Jason, who ironically, was my agent as well. They sent out a crew to Rochester, Washington and we filmed the tiny house adventure—Season 3, Episode 14.

That's how I officially became "The Tiny Home Guy." Now I was able to use the tagline "As seen on HGTV" in marketing my business. I ended up participating in four episodes for the show, one where we sold Christina her actual tiny home and another three where my products were used as decoys. Since the show is actually a reenactment, "decoy" - tiny homes are used as options in the episode that are either - "too big" or "too small" or "too blue " or whatever. Then, the one that they'd already picked before filming becomes "just right."

But if you go on HGTV and watch the aforementioned episode with Christina, you will notice that it's not me that's selling them their tiny home. It's a woman named Colleen.

Chapter 9: Colleen

Another business endeavor I experimented with was starting a driving school. A lot of people wanted to buy RVs but were afraid to drive them. I set up a school, taught people how to drive RVs and got them certified so they could get better rates on insurance. I was doing all of this on top of my RV dealership and raising two kids, so naturally, I needed help. That's where Colleen came in.

I had told myself I'd never marry a woman I met in a bar again, but I never said I couldn't hire one. I met Colleen at a bar in Vancouver, Washington. I walked in and saw her sitting alone at a table for two and asked her to dance. She was married and she wasn't my type; I don't think we even exchanged phone numbers. Then I saw her again at a happy hour place on the Columbia River. We struck up a conversation and she discovered I had children. I needed a babysitter at the time and she became Mary Poppins for my kids.

Then she started helping out with the driving school. After I got into the garden shed business, without yet knowing they were tiny homes, she handled all of the importing and exporting, facilitated everything with the distributors in Europe, and handled freight. I was just PR and sales, and she did everything in the back that you could imagine and more.

Colleen was a connector. She loved to strike up conversations with new people. We were at a show once at the fairgrounds in Salem, Oregon that was all about off-grid green products. I was invited to take my tiny house there. Colleen and I were teaching children how to build tiny homes when somebody from another display said, "Are you going to the tiny home show in Colorado Springs?" I said, "I've never heard about a show in Colorado." She told me it might be too late to register, but it was worth a try. I gave her my card and she made a call on my behalf.

The show promoter for what was called the Tiny Home Jamboree phoned and said, "We have 10,000 people registered from all over the world for this tiny home show."

"Really?" I said, pretty sure that number was inflated. "I've done over 400 trade shows in my career and I've had a lot of promoters tell me big numbers, but really? Ten thousand people from all over the world? We can't get people from all over the state to show up at a show, let alone the world."

She said, "Yes, it's true. We have people from Germany and Australia and many other countries registered."

I did the math; I took 25% of 10,000, still figuring the number was inflated. If 2,500 people came to see my tiny home, it would be worth it, I decided. So, I took two 20-foot tiny homes to Colorado Springs in August of 2015. There would be only about ten tiny homes for the thousands to view, in total.

The show was held in a field outside of the Western Museum of Mining and Industry, a little museum designed for small events. It was next to Bass Pro Shops, which was going to hold overflow parking if needed. It was needed. Sixty-thousand people showed up to the show over the three-day weekend. On the first day, 350 people were towed off the interstate because there was not enough parking. People were running through the field to see tiny homes as their cars were getting towed away by the hundreds.

The show was only supposed to be open during the mining museum's hours. The museum closed at 6 p.m.; imagine getting thousands of people to leave, who had been waiting in line for hours to see inside a tiny home. It was worse than Disneyland; there was no ride at the end. People would spend ninety seconds looking at a tiny home and then have to go get in another line and wait for hours to see the next one.

I've been in the RV business for four decades and I've never seen anything like it. They had loudspeakers telling people they had to leave, causing a small riot. I think some of the attendees may have been on drugs. It was like a little tiny home Woodstock.

The next day was a little more organized. They had shuttles operating from Bass Pro Shop, bringing people to the Western Mining Museum to see the tiny homes. All in all, it was an amazing show. I met a lot of really great people who I've done quite a bit of business with over the years. The tiny home world of do-it-yourselfers is just like any niche industry; it's really tight, everybody seems to know each other.

Colleen was at that show with me and met somebody that would stay in our lives. We were staying at the Garden of the Gods RV Park, which was a few miles away from the event, when Colleen saw somebody at the campground snooping in our tiny homes. We were parked close to a restroom and shower facility and someone getting out of the shower became curious.

"Would you like to look inside?" Colleen offered. "Oh, you caught me," the woman said. "I'm really sorry if I'm prowling." Colleen, being Colleen, said, "No, it's okay. Come on in and I'll tell you all about it."

We were setting up dealers at that point. The woman and her husband were retired, traveling in their RV, but they wanted to go to the tiny home show. They had pre-registered, but the show was so overcrowded they didn't get to see my tiny homes at the show, so they were grateful for the private showing. After they were done with the tour and talking to me about tiny homes, they decided that they wanted to become dealers in their home state of Vermont.

After the show, they ended up following me to Washington State, where they decided to build their own tiny house on a trailer. They stayed at my RV lot until the tiny home was road-ready, and then took the rest of their

United States tour in their new tiny home.

Due to the success of the Tiny Home Jamboree's first year, there was no doubt the organizers would host another one. The show returned to Colorado Springs the following year. I was all set to have a couple more tiny homes on display when Colleen became very ill. She went to the doctor and was diagnosed with brain cancer.

The news was devastating. But nowhere in my mind did I think it was fatal. I had survived cancer myself and Colleen was a tough woman. Still, I wanted to be with her during the treatment. But Colleen insisted, "The show must go on. I'm going to be okay. Don't stay here at the hospital with me. I have family with me; I'm in a good spot. Just go." I wanted to argue with her, but I respected her wishes. So, I left.

That's when I decided to take my daughter along to celebrate her eighteenth birthday. I was planning to celebrate on the way to the event while towing behind the Tour Bus, a newly designed creation that wasn't even started five days before leaving for the Colorado Jamboree. On Monday, one of our sales gals, who would end up traveling with us, asked where the unit was that we were taking for her to show. I pointed to my head and said, "It's in here."

The sales girl quizzed me, "What do you mean, it's not built yet?" I answered matter of factly, "We are starting on it today." She asked one more question to get the facts straight in her mind. "Aren't you leaving on Saturday?

This is Monday." Yep, she had it right. "You are correct."

We headed down the street with the trailer to reinforce the hitch. This was going to be my biggest display ever, a real showstopper at the Colorado show. It was a thirty-six-foot beauty we built with long hours every day and into the night. On Saturday morning, when we pulled out, the stain was still drying. We headed south to the Dunes in Oregon to meet a tiny house client. We found furniture along the way to put into the unit, which had two-bedroom lofts, a king and a queen, with a downstairs entry porch as well as a BBQ porch on the upper deck. It also had a small shop/storage area near the bathroom located at the back.

Next stop, Sacramento. We pulled over near the In-N-Out Burger along Interstate 80, where we picked up the sales girl, who would join us to try to fill the big tiny house showing shoes of Colleen. When we arrived at Colorado Springs, we set up by day and shopped all night at twenty-four-hour box stores to fill the Big Tiny Home with furnishings. We chose a bicycle theme, "Enjoy the Adventure."

When the doors opened, we were ready! We had turned heads while driving at eighty miles per hour on the way to the Jamboree, now we were turning heads in Colorado. On opening day, it was decided the lines to get inside were so long that we needed to stop the viewers from turning around inside the unit. We cut a doorway in the kitchen wall to allow the Tiny Home Zombies to enter on the lower patio and exit out the bathroom/former shop door. Our sales girl, a math and science teacher on summer break, kept a tally sheet. For every fifteen minutes, we showed our Big Tiny to 225 tiny house enthusiasts who did nothing but *oooooh* and *ahhhhh* all the way through.

It was now Sunday, August 7, 2016 - the final day of the show. At first, it was just another show day. I got up, went to my display and started giving tours. Then, Tom and Diane came over—the couple we had met at the campground during the previous year's show. "I'm so sorry about Colleen," they said. "What do you mean?" I asked, although I figured they were referring to her not having been able to be here, because of her illness. "We saw the news on Face book - she passed away early this morning, we thought you knew..."

It was only thirty days after her diagnosis. I had never considered her situation would come to this. I was in shock. And I still had the rest of the show day to make it through. I left my display to have it speak for itself. I just wandered aimlessly throughout the show for the rest of the day. At closing time, I took the tiny home and drove it around the country for the next fifty-two days. I couldn't go home. I couldn't go back to work.

There was no real saving grace for a situation like that, but I am grateful for one thing: Colleen got to see herself on TV before she passed. She was so excited about that HGTV episode, which wasn't scheduled to air until November. When HGTV found out she was sick, they aired it early—just a few days before she passed away. She was the Vanna White of our episode, the tour guide showing Christina all the different tiny homes -that had to have made her smile.

Colleen was a very special woman. She was a positive influence on my children and a great supporter of me personally and my businesses. I really miss her and I never tried to replace her - she's irreplaceable.

Chapter 10:
Ken Con

Colleen introduced me to a lot of nice people that contributed to my life in positive ways. Ken Con wasn't one of them.

Once upon a time, in 2015, Colleen was at a tiny home show with me when she said, "I met this person that has an amazing water product." I told her, "Colleen, stop right there, I'm not interested in anything that has to do with water - I'm too busy for water," I said. She insisted, "You really need to talk to him, please, just meet him."..... I still refused.

A few weeks later, while Coleen and I were working on the patio of our satellite office in Jantzen Beach, Oregon, a guy with short pants and little boots strolled over. My initial instinct was to avoid him, but Coleen stood up and said, "Oh, hi, this is Blair." He's the one I was telling you about. I thought to myself, Oh no, it's the water guy. She had set me up, and she had.

We got to talking and the guy (whose name I've changed to "Con" to protect the guilty) was so good at selling his product that, I thought, you know what, we might have something here.

The product was a miniaturized water purification

system. The more I learned about the product, I thought, that's kind of cool. Then it got better the more he explained just what could be accomplished by catching rain water and turning it into usable water in many ways in the tiny home. I figured I could sell it as an upgrade to my tiny homes and I need a water system anyway, why not do this?

Then the "Con" said, "If I could just follow you around everywhere you go, I could sell these and do quite well." The part of me that likes to be everyone's buddy said, "Yes. Come join me!" So, he tagged along with me to shows and we put one of his water purification systems in my tiny home. He sold quite a few of them in concept, which led me to decide to open up a tiny home manufacturing facility with the intention of creating this tiny home package deal. Through connections I had, I was even able to promote the tiny homes with water systems on *Good Morning America*.

The punch line is, I sold a few of these systems to find out that in reality, the product didn't even exist. It existed for skyscrapers and residential, but it had never been miniaturized to adapt to a tiny home. In theory, it would work. But because they didn't have the proof of concept money, they never miniaturized it. I got conned by the "Con."

I was fraudulently induced into starting a company with a guy that was not even the owner of the company. He was a rep for another company out of Germany that was run out of a company based in Florida. I found out by calling the owner of the company in Florida that he was only allowed to market the product for residential homes in the Pacific Northwest and that he wasn't even selling it by the name of the actual product.

After I promoted and sold the product and came to find out that they could not deliver, I had to give refunds. This created a big problem because I was attempting to put an agreement together (with a man that the Con had introduced me to), essentially merging a couple of different companies and then take that company public.

When I found out the water product wasn't even real, I sent a warning message to the rest of the potential shareholders, explaining what had happened. Within three hours, I was sent an email that my services were no longer needed. The new company had "decided to go in a different direction." I was asked to return all keys, information leads and even my tiny home assets over to the new company, which I had created but was now no longer a part of.

There's a lot I could say about what happened next, but the bottom line is that by the time I filed a civil multi-million-dollar lawsuit the new company had gone bankrupt. Meanwhile, I was bled down to just about nothing. I invested a lot of energy into getting back what I had lost, only to realize, two years later, that I could make new money faster than it would take to win back the money I had lost—with a hell of a lot less stress.

Sure, the Con and his cronies interrupted the flow I had going with my tiny home business; they took all of my manufacturing kits and I had to try to survive with just my RV business for a while. I wouldn't be "the tiny home guy" anymore. But success is the best form of revenge. Two years later, they're still going through bankruptcy and I've built my tiny home business back up, beyond the level that it was then (more on that in the next chapter). Plus, I've learned some valuable lessons:

#1 – Do your due diligence before going into business with someone. I would have discovered he was just a rep and a fraud.

#2 – Don't get involved in a pity party. It's easier to move forward and start over than to go back and fight.

#3 – As the saying goes, keep your friends close and your enemies closer. I was too naïve and too transparent.

#4 – Trust your gut. I had all kinds of warnings that the Con was not someone worth trusting that I unfortunately ignored.

#5 – Trust your friends. I had five high-level people tell me not to go into business with him. One of them was a close mentor. He must have done some kind of a background check and tried to ease me into his realistic premonitions. I got too excited about the vision that I stopped listening to reasonable voices.

Colleen meant well when she introduced me to the Con. Maybe, rest her soul, she knew better than I did—he would teach me lessons I needed to learn. But, I think from now on, I will be better served if I listen to my mentor. He is the one that fondly called me the Godfather of Tiny Homes, yet he is the one that really taught me very important tiny house driving lessons to help me move forward, steering me away from disaster.

Chapter 11:
Envisioning the Future

My business goal for this year is to have manufacturing facilities providing products for different variations of tiny home needs, whether it be for emergency disaster relief (fire, flood, hurricane, tornado, mudslides), or affordable housing initiatives for the homeless. There are also a lot of people that aren't homeless but need to downsize to have a more manageable space.

Parents and grandparents are interested in tiny homes because what they had or have is too big for what they need. A lot of young people don't want to handle the stress of large homes anymore, whether they can afford a large home or not. There is a new generation of minimalists that don't want to waste money buying more stuff.

Tiny homes are the answer to a lot of people's desire to get away from the big man chains—the rat race, big mortgages. I've heard it so many times, "Wow, if I could get out of this house, this larger home and big mortgage. I've heard it so many times; I would have peace and freedom."

Then we also have a lot of customers where Mom and Dad are moving in with the kids, or the kids are moving in with Mom and Dad, into homes without enough space. They think *if we could just get something small so they could have their own space, but not be in our place.* Those customers make up a big part of the tiny home movement.

As for my passion for veterans and the homeless is being expressed through our company. There are veterans who are on re-entry plans that could use the happiness that a tiny home offers. When enthusiasts see tiny homes on HGTV, they see glamour—they don't see the homeless. But there's an opportunity with tiny homes to help humanity.

The idea is to have tiny home communities for the homeless, where residents go through a four-step program. They can push their shopping cart right up to the tiny home, check into it, get undercover (whether it's rain, heat or whatever), take a shower, get medication, and so forth. Then they're taken through a drying out period or interview process to find out if they're willing and want to be retrained and go to work. If they are, then they can go to step two and start some training and get job placements and if that works well, they go to step three, which is a different house.

A lot of the homeless aren't just single guys lying on the sidewalk. They are families. Some are really trying to figure out how to integrate back into society. They are working homeless; their income just isn't enough for them to be able to afford rent or a mortgage. They need something where they can feel good about themselves. They need some privacy. Tiny homes are a great alternative for them to move into, get their lives together, and then move out.

Through these initiatives, we hope to create opportunities for the homeless, veterans, and other groups to accommodate a variety of housing needs across the United States and beyond. Once one city proves successful with this type of investment for the homeless, then the program can be duplicated all over the United States and elsewhere. Once the "proof of concept" is there, other cities and governments follow suit.

I've always been a pioneer in whatever I've done, whether it's in the RV industry or the tiny home movement. I'm an icebreaker; when big chunks break open, I say, "Yeah, its working!" Then it flows down the river and gets caught on other ice. Then my team and I break the ice up again and again until finally, the path is cleared.

As the tiny home movement progresses, for me personally, I see myself moving into a big mansion somewhere with all my toys and my helicopter and boat and submarine. And if I get tired of those things, then I'll go to my treehouse in Belize with my zip line to the beach. I can run the company from anywhere in the world, as long as I have a cell phone or a laptop. I've already beaten the streets and toured everywhere..... now it's my team's job to sell, manufacture, and deliver all the promises that I've made.

Along the way, I've learned that the secret to being number one is making everyone else number one. I've always worked hard to help other people thrive. If you help enough people become successful, you will never need to worry about how you're going to make it in the world. I can sleep at night because I feel I'm contributing some good to the world.

Now, the tiny home movement has become a machine that can't be stopped—with me or without me. It was on a popular trajectory before anyone knew what a corona virus was, but the economic uncertainty of recent times has made living tiny all the more attractive. People are taking different directions and making adjustments to their lives.

It doesn't matter how many commas and zeros someone has in their financial statement, the reaction a tiny home evokes is the same—joy and enthusiasm, whether they want to buy one for themselves or not. Throughout the hundreds of thousands of miles I've driven my tiny home around the country, it has made people smile.

My tiny home has served me like a VIP pass; wherever I pull up, the red carpet rolls out and I am welcomed—from the glitzy streets of Las Vegas to the Tiny Street of Dreams in Daytona Beach, Florida and Sturgis, South Dakota, to Cave Creek, Arizona. The most amazing people I've met in my life over the last decade have come through having a tiny home. I feel like a celebrity, even if no one knows my name. I'm "The Tiny Home Guy," and that is a title I hold proudly.

Chapter 12:
What the Family Thinks

Memories of My Son

Ron was always ambitious, curious and intelligent, with way too much energy that needed to be redirected.

When he was 5 years old we lived on a cul-de-sac in an English village. He had no friends because English boys were not allowed to play with American boys with long blue jeans. Ron made friends with the milkman, who would pick him at the corner of the cul-de-sac and then allowed Ron to deliver the milk to each home and then drop him off on his way home.

That was his first business endeavor.

We were stationed at Weatherford Air Force Base in England at the time. Some American Airmen had bought land from a mushroom farmer near the airbase to build Tiny Homes. The purpose for these Tiny Homes was to bring their families over to England. Ron loved living in the Tiny homes because he could play with the kids who also lived in the neighborhood.

Ron graduated at the age of 17 with several opportunities. When he was 18 he met a man who saw potential in him to sell real estate. He put all of his focus and energy into passing the real estate test and said it was harder than passing the bar exam that an attorney would have to take. He passed his Real Estate test and got his license. He went off to sell real estate. In short time he became their top salesman and broke all sales records for his division in the company.

After Ron's experience selling real estate, one of his friends asked if he would come to work selling recreational vehicles. After a 13 year experience at this particular RV dealership he decided to open up his own dealerships.

As time went on, Ron opened up 3 different locations and had job opportunities for family and acquaintance. After I retired he had a job for me working the booths at the RV shows.

When you buy a recreational vehicle or a tiny home from Ron- you also get a friend for life. I could write a book about all the friends that Ron still has because they bought something from him.

I am very proud and honored to be the mother of such a hard working, kind and well thought of and creative person.

Memories of Dad

One of my earliest memories of my dad is when he taught me how to draw a heart. My dad is the one who taught me how to draw certain shapes and the shape that stuck is the heart, which

was really fitting considering he is one of the most loving and caring people I have ever known. He taught me to spell my name, Demi, with a heart on top of the "I," and to this day I still write my name that way.

A favorite memory of mine is from back when I was maybe five or six. I would play the video game The Legend of Zelda Ocarina of Time. In the game, I would run around gathering the things I needed and solving puzzles until I got to the part when I had to fight the first boss, which is a big tough enemy I called "The Spider." It was so scary for me that I refused to fight it and would ask Dad to fight it for me. He fought it several times for me because I was never able to get very far after he defeated it, so I'd start over and get to the spider and say "Dad, fight the spider!" and make him fight it again. One time when dad was fighting it, all of a sudden, the phone rang and Dad abruptly got up, tossing the controller in my lap with the game un-paused as he walked away to answer the phone. Panic surged through me as I saw the spider approach me on the screen, but I remembered every move my dad made when he fought it all the times before and I mimicked what he would have done and ended up defeating it! It was my first time killing the boss. I was so excited and I wasn't scared of any of the monsters anymore.

Another of my very early memories is of sitting on my dad's lap in my parents' bedroom. He was crying a little, telling me in what was attempted to be a composed voice, that he couldn't live at home anymore. My parents fought for as long as I could remember and I didn't think they should be together anyways, but I was still sad because I didn't want my dad to leave. I had a much better relationship with him than I ever did with my mom, and still do.

Sometime after Dad moved out, it was Easter Sunday and he had come to the house to give me and my sister De'Aunna Easter presents. I remember getting a very large stuffed bunny. My mom was yelling at my dad for whatever reason (it never mattered what, there seemed to always be a reason for mom to be angry with Dad). I never understood why she hated him so much when he always tried to make everyone happy and laugh. The end result of that encounter was me sitting on the stairs leading halfway up to our bedrooms, hugging my new stuffed bunny tight, quietly sobbing as I listened to Mom continue to scream at Dad from the front door of the house, telling him to leave the property before she called the cops again (she would always make up some reason to call the cops).

The day Dad was going to tell Mom that he wanted a divorce was only after a short time of being married to her. They went to a restaurant and both had news they wanted to share. Mom shared her news first and told him that she was pregnant (with me). Right then, Dad decided not to tell Mom he wanted a divorce anymore because he wanted to stay to be with his child. I often wonder how different things would have been if Dad had shared his news first. I feel bad because, in a way, my existence trapped him into many more years of misery with Mom, but I am also glad that he didn't leave because I needed him and would never have made it through a childhood of mental and emotional abuse from my Mom without the affection, joy, and laughter he brought me through all of my sadness. Even though my mom was awful to my dad, he stayed with her as long as he could so he could be with us.

He taught us to speak kindly even when we were angry by reminding us to "speak with love in your voice." I would wonder why he'd tell us to be nice to our mom when Mom only-said awful things about him. I wondered how he could still be so kind and joyful. His positive attitude is one of his best features and something I still aspire to apply to my life.

Dad also taught us that "You become what you think about," which helps to focus your attention on your thoughts. If you think angry thoughts, you'll probably feel angry too. Same goes with positive thoughts, you'll end up feeling more positive feelings.

When my sister and I were kids we used to play this game called "kick the can." There is one person who defends the can from being kicked and the other two would try to run and kick the can without getting tagged. I remember Dad was so fast that I'd get scared when I saw him coming, he was really good at that game, but Dad is really good at everything he does.

We have a family tradition of playing croquet. Dad taught us and many others how to play. He'd be patient and kind, showing us how to hold the mallet and where to aim and how to strategize. He made us into really good players but he is still difficult to beat.

Dad would get up in the middle of the night and eat ice cream. He had so much ice cream in the freezer that I would tell him it's like a mini Baskin Robbins in there. He also puts peanut butter on so many different things and bakes Cheerios or puts them in a skillet and drizzles butter on them. I get my strange snacking habits from Dad.

Dad has always had trouble getting enough sleep. He works so hard that I sometimes found him asleep in the middle of typing an email and he almost always passes out during a movie, even in the movie theaters! I've had to nudge him with my elbow to get him to wake up because he was starting to snore in the theater! One night, Dad thought he heard someone yelling "Dad!" over and over. He went outside and discovered it wasn't a distressed child at all; it was just the neighbor's goat.

Every year, around December, Dad would randomly sing Christmas songs while he cooked, cleaned, or drove somewhere. I was usually grumpy, but my dad's cheerfulness would snap me out of it. We would decorate new Christmas stockings every couple of years and use all manner of craft supplies. It got to be a bit much when he bought giant stockings nearly the size of a person.

My dad can be very silly and does a lot of Jim Carrey impressions. Dad would mess around in the car and when he would be close to taking a turn, he would pretend to turn the wheel, sliding his hands over it, like he was spinning it really fast but it wouldn't go anywhere. He would suddenly go, "Oh no!" and I'd gasp worriedly and ask "What's wrong?!" and then he'd cheerfully say "Just practicing my 'oh no's." Eventually, I wouldn't get worried anymore when he'd do it, I'd just give him a look.

Dad let us have several cats even though he insisted he didn't like cats and would call them "bad dogs." He would sometimes say that they had a "good paint job" though, referring to their fur patterns. I had one cat named Shadow. Dad would throw dice across the room and Shadow would go pick them up and bring them back; basically, he'd play fetch with the cat.

Throughout my life, Dad would leave a note for whatever reason, usually to say goodbye and have a nice day, if he had to leave before I would wake up. He always put a big smiley face and a "Love, Dad" at the end.

My dad taught me over the years how to be a good house-spouse, how to cook French toast, how to clean and how to take care of a car. I get most of my advice from him. He doesn't always know how to help me because he can't understand all my challenges of what I'm going through, but he tries his best to be patient and give me advice according to what he knows and comes up with some wisdom to give me.

Growing up, he gave us a lot of freedom to make our own decisions and space to express ourselves, resulting in some interesting art, music, and fashion choices over the years but he never tried to control us or make us think a certain way. The time I had to myself make my imagination grow and creativity flourish.

For one Father's Day, when I was a teenager, my dad's girlfriend at the time had this idea that my sister De'Aunna and I could make a box that contained a bunch of folded up note cards that we could fill with kind words and memories we had for Dad. We got a small wooden chest with a metal clasp and painted it all black with a red trim (black and red is one of Dad's favorite color schemes) and red hearts all over it (he likes hearts). We split up some purple note cards and slowly filled each one out and put a red heart at the end of each sentence or paragraph. We also put a handful of little red paper hearts in the box in the folded-up notes. When we did end up giving the box to Dad, he sat on a chair and started pulling out one note to read at a time while we sat on the floor of the living room and watched. He would read one out loud and either "aww" or laugh, but when he got to a particularly deep and heartfelt one, his voice started to change and I could tell he was trying not to get emotional. We had made him so happy and I was glad because he really is the best dad ever. (The box remains in his office to this day.)

One of the note cards from the box was written by me and said: "Even though Mom had convinced me you were a bad guy and I didn't want to live anymore, you never gave up on me and you pulled me through the darkness and into the light."

My dad is my hero because he kept me alive during my darkest times. He rescued me from my mom. He's always been there when we needed him from the very beginning. He always provided for us what we needed and tried to make our time together fun, whenever he wasn't working. He put in so many long hours for all of us and made the time with us quality time.

My dad bought me beautiful flowers and a butterfly corsage on my wedding day. I was having a bare minimum elopement ceremony in our backyard and didn't want anything for decorations, but he spent all this time wrapping these flowers together into a wonderful bouquet. With all the thought and love he put into it, I caved and decided to hold it during the ceremony. Dad made a last-minute decision to ask if he could walk me to the altar (which was just a decorated garden arch). Even though there was no aisle and we only had two other people to witness, I said yes. He looked so happy; it was so sweet. At some point during the ceremony, he cried a little; my spouse told me he saw it and Dad denied it but it made me happy to know.

My favorite quote my dad taught me that I think about all the time is, "Take the best and leave the rest." I like it so much because it can be applied to anything, but I especially like it when it comes to learning new ideas. I don't have to buy into everything someone is teaching but I can take the parts that I think are good or I can apply to my life, and the other stuff I'm not such a fan of, I can simply leave behind.

Memories from DeAunna

Without going into too much detail, my life had a lot of ups and downs. I moved in with my Dad when I was around 14 to our childhood home in Rochester, WA. At the time I had only seen my Dad over the years between planned weekend visits and holidays, birthdays etc. So when I was officially living there it was challenging at first. As I felt I did not know him really well - but, I loved him and it was definitely a change from only ever living with my Mom.

I had my fair share of "acting out" moments in the years following that transition.

My Dad taught me some valuable lessons.

He continued to trust me and gave me the benefit of the doubt even when I probably didn't deserve it. After skipping countless weeks of high school he treated me with respect and gave me my privacy. He let me learn, grow, make mistakes and mature on my own without trying to mold me into what "he" expected of me. He just loved me as me and was always there with solutions when mistakes were made or when things got rocky.

When I really reflect, all of my most memorable and cherished memories are of being at my Dads - from summer camping trips to days on the lake doing water sports with family friends.

A lot of the independence I had as a girl and even now as an adult, I learned from him. He taught me to make pancakes; cook Kraft Mac and cheese as well as many other adventures were experienced with my Dad.

Some of my best memories are from when I was around 16, getting to travel the country side with my Dad going state to state. I even started collecting key chains from each state so I could remember the trips. I have now collected about 10 different souvenirs from the States traveled.

On those road trips I was helping with the tiny house shows, spending a great deal of time talking away with my Dad and watching States go by. We went through the Redwood Forest along the coast of Oregon-California, viewing amazingly huge bloodstained trees. We stopped in the gift shop and I purchased a jewelry box made from the redwood trees. I even had my sweet 16 Birthday - on the road in the RV with a chocolate ice cream cake.

As the rebellious kid I was - my sweet 16 request was my first tattoo - which I got in Flagstaff Arizona, a cute little mountain town and I remember it starting to snow as we left that night. That first road trip was quite an experience.

Our second trip together was mostly the same route. I was just turning 18 and once again, as a birthday request, my Dad went in half with me on my 2nd tattoo. It is actually still my favorite-even after dozens of tattoos later. I selected a big dragon tattooed on my back when passing through Denver, Colorado. Through the whole three and half hour process, he would stop in with his smile - taking a zillion photos (a Dad-right)?

When we arrived in New Mexico, Dad would sit on top of the RV with me and hunt for 'UFO'S among the stars. Absolutely a favorite memory, it was a perfect pitch black sky, dazzling with millions of stars untouched by the glow of city lights.

Dad always made everything so much fun, maybe because he is also one to bend the rules and do his own thing. I learned a lot on those trips and it was really great father-daughter bonding experiences.

I remember when my Dad was building the "Tiny Street of Dreams" and he let me help build one of the first tiny homes in Washington State. I enjoyed it so much; it was interestingly easy-because it was like Lego's. He taught me everything I know about building and "MacGyvering" as we say. Even now I can fix broken cabinets in my own home.

With teaching me so much and always being there when we needed it - no one can compare to ~the~ Ron Blair. Always juggling 20 tasks at once and would put it all on hold to stop and come to the rescue.

After giving birth to my daughter in 2018 at 20 years of age, I moved to Oahu, Hawaii with my husband who was active duty USMC. We lived there approximately 3 years, learning to be our own family in the military, which was riddled with its own challenges.

My husband finished his military contract and is an honorable veteran and we have a beautiful daughter who just turned 3. We are back home in Washington State, where my daughter gets to have a relationship with both sides of our family and can experience living in her birth State.

My Dad picked us up the day we landed and even had a whole bedroom area already set up for our arrival. We stayed almost a month during our transition to getting our new home.

My Dad and my daughter, Alahya, were able to make up for all the missed quality time from being thousands of miles apart.

It warms my heart when they're both snuggled up watching movies - making him the best Grandpa on Earth!